Letters for my little angels

Nicole Hinton

To order additional copies of this book, contact:
Xlibris
844-714-8691
www.Xlibris.com
Orders@Xlibris.com

Scripture taken from the King James Version of the Bible.

ISBN:	Softcover	978-1-6641-7480-1
	Hardcover	978-1-6641-7481-8
	EBook	978-1-6641-7479-5

Library of Congress Control Number: 2021909818

Print information available on the last page

Rev. date: 05/17/2021

Chapter 1

Fear Not, Little One

When you first get the diagnosis from your doctor, it can be scary. When you feel that tight knot in your stomach, the fear inside your heart is overwhelming. Sometimes you may need to cry and shed a tear or two. Do not feel ashamed if you do; sometimes you need to cry to let it out. It is okay. I know that diagnosis can make you fearful, not knowing what will happen next. You may need a great big hug as tight as possible to help you cope, and that's okay. You may cry a little more on your pillow at night. That is okay too. I will be your shoulder to lean on, and I will wipe your tears away. Do not be afraid, for I am always with you. While dreams dance around in your head and you awake the next morning and step out of bed, look out of the window and gaze. Watch the beautiful sunrays and the singing blue jays. Remember this message.

"The Lord is my light and my salvation; whom shall I fear? The Lord is the strength of my life; of whom shall I be afraid?" (Psalm 27:1). I will place my shield of protection around you. When the lights go out and you are comfy in your bed, look out of your window and see the bright stars up the sky. I made each of them light up to make a display just for you—the Little Dipper, the Big Dipper, the Great Bear, and the North Star too. But none of those stars are as bright as you. Fear not, for you are always under my watch. I will be with you even while you dream.

Chapter 2

You Are Strong

ou may be small, but you are very strong .You can do anything. When at first you don't succeed, try and try again. You may not be as big as a dinosaur or as fast as a cheetah, but a little confidence is all you need, and all you have to do is believe in yourself. You are growing stronger every day. You have the strength to move mountains. To stay strong, you must eat a heathy diet with plenty of fruit and veggies and get plenty of rest and exercise. You are just like little David when he killed Goliath. The giant even thought he was much smaller, and Goliath was bigger. You may face a terrible disease that may seem big and scary like a monster! You can face that disease and be brave just like little David.

"I can do all things through Christ which strengtheneth me" (Philippians 4:13).

"The Lord is my strength and song, and is become my salvation" (Psalm 118:14)

My little angel, you are very strong and courageous. Sometimes you may get sick and have to go to the hospital, and that is okay. I am always with you, and we will get through this together. You are more strong at heart when you are at your weakest, then you find your inner strength. And you realize that you were stronger than you thought you were, and you find a strength you never knew you had .You can do it. I know you can.

Chapter 3

You Are Not Alone

Sometimes when you go to the hospital, you may feel all alone. Some kids may have a mommy or a daddy to go to the hospital with them. Some kids only have one parent or may have adoptive parents. Some kids have no parents at all and have to wait to be adopted to a family. Every child wants to feel that they are not alone. It is okay to feel lonely sometimes. "Turn to me and be gracious. Have mercy upon me, oh Lord, for I am lonely and afflicted" (Psalm 25:16). He is a father to the fatherless. He is a mother to the motherless. He is a friend who sticketh closer than a brother. "As for me, I will behold thy face in righteousness: I shall be satisfied when I awake, with thy likeness" (Psalm 17:15).

"For lo, I am with you always, even unto the end of the world"

(Matthew 28:20). Do not feel lonely, my child. You are not alone. I will be with you. When you lay in your hospital bed and look out the window and see the bright sun shine and hear the songs of colorful birds singing or see beautiful rainbows, just know that it is me bringing you rays of happiness. I will be your pillow and shoulder to lie on. I will give you sweet dreams at night. I will be your friend, mother, sister, and brother. I will be your blanket of comfort to hug you tight. I will always be with you. You are never alone.

Sometimes when you are in the hospital, the doctor may have to apply medicine to you. You may have to have a surgery. It can be scary and hard to trust that everything will be okay. You may have to go to the doctor for your first checkup. You may feel nervous, and you may have to have a shot. Ouch! Shots can be painful, but you must trust and know that as long as Mom or Dad holds your hand, everything will be okay. You may have to take a breath and count down before your shot .You can think of something happy. Think of your favorite ice cream or your favorite toy. Think about the crystal blue colors of the oceans. Think about the beautiful colors of the birds and the orange and red leaves in the fall. I designed them all. Having trust can take a small step, but it can be a huge leap. You can do it. "Trust in the Lord with all thine heart, and lean not unto thine own understanding. In all thy ways, acknowledge him, and he shall direct thy paths" (Proverbs 3:5–6). Trust me, everything will be okay, my little angel.

Chapter 5

You Are Beautiful

"I will praise thee, for I am fearfully and wonderfully made" (Psalm 139:14). My child, you are perfect in every way .From the crown of your head to the tip of your feet, they are made just right for you. From the day you were born, as you laid for nine months in your mother's womb, I already knew your name. It was sewn into the palms of your hands. I wrapped you in a beautiful blanket of skin. I shaped your bones together just right altogether and in place. I placed two perfect pearls of eyes inside your two sockets. I gave you two little hands, and you have five little fingers on each hand .I gave you two strong legs and two adorable feet, and I gave you five toes on each feet. I even know what you are thinking and when you feel scared and when you feel sad. I placed a beautiful nose right in the middle of your face, and best of all, I gave you the biggest smile to share and brighten up the world. You were made, shaped, and adorned in my image, and I beheld you, and you were and will always be perfect in my eyesight .My dear beloved child, you are beautiful and adorned by me.

Chapter 6
Letter for Comfort

I know that what you are going through can be tough. It is hard to spend those nights alone in a hospital room. Have no fear, my little angel. This is my message for you. When thy passest through the waters, I will be with thee, and through the rivers, they shall not overflow thee. When thou walkest through the fire, thou shalt not be burned; neither shall the flame kindle upon thee (Isaiah 42:9). When you need someone to give you that great big hug or when you just need a laugh or you need someone to cuddle you up in their arms just right, I will wrap you in the safety of my arms. I will cuddle you in the lonely nights. When you toss in your bed and dream sweet dreams, you will float on the dust of my cloud. I will whisper softly in your ears and sing sweet lullabies, just to comfort you and let you know that everything will be all right. I will awake you in the mornings with my sunshine, and you will look into the morning sky and see the bright sun rise and hear the sweet hymns from the birds and see beautiful flowers and colorful butterflies, and you will know that I did it all for you. My child, I will be with you, for I will be your comfort, and remember, I love you always to infinity.

Chapter 7

There Is Hope

When the doctor walks in to the room to deliver the bad news to you that they have done all that they can do, it may seem as if all is lost. It is not the end for you but only the beginning. You are a fighter, and you will get through this. Remember going fishing and jumping in the mud puddles. Remember riding the swing sets up and down and sliding down the slide board. You can do it. Just place one step in front of the other, and then you will be running. If at first you don't succeed, try and try again. This I recall to my mind, therefore have I hope. The Lord is my portion, saith my soul. Therefore will I hope in him (Lamentations 3 21–24). "Withhold not thy tender mercies from me, O Lord: let thy lovingkindness and thy truth continually preserve me (Psalm 40:11).

"As the harp panteth after the water brooks, so panteth my soul after thee, O God" (Psalm 42:1). My child, there is hope. Do not be dismayed. You are a fighter, my little angel.

Chapter 8

You Can Conquer Anything

Yes, you did it! You made it through your surgery. After your surgery, you may have to learn to walk again. You may have one leg, and the other may be a prosthetic, but you can do anything. You may have had a brain surgery, but you made it this far. Do not give up now. You are almost at the finish line. I am proud of you .With lots of love and support from loved ones, all you have to do is go through your therapy and recovery sessions. Exercise with your therapist. They are here to help you get better. Remember you can do it. Practice, practice. "Nay, in all these things we are more than conquerors through him that loved us" (Romans 8:37). "But thanks be to God, which giveth us the victory through our Lord Jesus Christ" (Romans 15:57). "But thou, O Lord art a shield for me; my glory, and the lifter up of mine head" (Psalm 3:3). Look at you now. Be glad and rejoice in confidence because you are a conqueror, and you can triumph over anything. You are victorious. You made it to the finish line. Congratulations! I knew you could do it. You can conquer anything!

Chapter 9

Sing and Be Happy

You can rejoice now! You can dance! You can sing and be happy! You can walk again! Just look at you now! Mom and Dad are proud of the steps you have made, and you should be too! Even if on days you do not feel so happy, you can sing a song, and it will make you feel much better. If you have a day that you are feeling low, just think back on the happy days. Remember those days when you have learned to walk again, and you made it through your therapy exercise, and the doctor says you can go home. You may not feel 100 percent on certain days. You can write a song about it. You can sing about anything! Mom and Dad may know some great songs to sing together with you. The therapist may also want to sing a song with you. You may not have the best voice in the bunch, but it is always okay to sing your way to a better place in your mind. Singing is a beautiful therapy. You can sing about sunshine or sing about rain. Sing about fluffy clouds that look like marshmallows. Sing of the mud puddles you love to jump in. Sing about your favorite foods you love to eat. A great song can always help brighten one's day. "Speaking to yourselves in psalms and hymns and spiritual songs, singing and making melody in your heart to the Lord" (Ephesians 5:19). My child, you can sing.

You Are a Winner

You have completed your course. You went through the cancer treatment and have made it to the end. You took your medicine like a brave little soldier, and you made it through your surgery. You walked without your walker through your therapy treatment. Look how far you have come! Look at the mountains you have climbed! Look at the valleys you toiled through! Many lonely days and dark nights you cried through .The pain you endured was unbearable, but you took it like a champ and that medicine tasted awful, yuck! Seizures are the worst. I know it is difficult at times, but keep taking the medicine, and they will keep them under control. Your loved ones are here for you. You won this! You can jump through hoops! Second Timothy 4:7 states, "I have fought the good fight, I have finished the race, I have kept the faith." My child, you have won your course. Amen.

Printed in the United States
by Baker & Taylor Publisher Services